# The New Mandolin

# Simon Mayor

## Acoustics

The New Mandolin
Simon Mayor

ISBN    0-9522776-0-3

Second edition 1994

First published in 1993 by
Acoustics (Publishing)
PO Box 350
Reading RG6 2DQ
Berkshire
England

All music, music transcriptions and accompanying text © Simon Mayor
Illustrations © 1993 Hilary James
Front cover photograph (SM with mandola by Mike Vanden) © Nigel Tribbeck

# CONTENTS

# A BIOGRAPHICAL NOTE

After a couple of years strumming a ukelele, Simon Mayor was given a guitar and the inevitable Bert Weedon tutor for his eleventh birthday. A few years later, hearing Irish fiddle music for the first time, he pestered the school music teacher for violin lessons, but was told he was too old! He decided to learn anyway, discovering the unlikely bedfellows of bluegrass and Vaughan Williams along the way. Hearing some rare recordings of 1930's mandolin orchestras he decided to try yet another instrument and found that the skills already acquired on the guitar (plectrum style) and the fiddle (which shares the same tuning) gave him a head start.

He has toured Britain from Orkney to Sark and played at festivals, theatres and arts centres throughout Europe and as far afield as Singapore. He is also a member of the band 'Slim Panatella and the Mellow Virginians', a Western Swing outfit which gives him the chance to let loose on some country swing fiddle as well as bluegrass mandolin.

With singer and double bass player Hilary James he has written topical songs which have provided light relief on serious news programmes. They have also written over fifty children's songs which have featured on many classic TV and radio programmes. A song collection, the 'Musical Mystery Tour', is published by Faber Music together with a CD and five tapes from Acoustics Records.

His long standing intention has been to write and record music specifically for the mandolin and exploit the possibilities of the instrument in the classical repertoire. His friendship with instrument maker Mike Vanden led to the construction of the mandola and mandocello, the larger and more unusual members of the mandolin family, instruments which offered even greater scope in writing and recording.

So with inspiration drawn from baroque music, 20th century British composers, traditional music, and the mandolin orchestras of the 1930s, he embarked upon *The Mandolin Album* mixing original tunes with inventive arrangements of the classics. Such was its success that *The Second Mandolin Album* and *Winter with Mandolins* followed soon after. All three albums have been embraced by national and local TV and radio - everywhere from specialist classical, folk and country programmes to the mainstream.

# THE NOTATION

The tunes are written in both conventional notation and tablature.

For those unfamiliar with tablature, it is an ancient and very simple method of notation, the four horizontal lines representing the strings (E at the top, G at the bottom), and the numbers indicating the frets to be fingered. Its great advantage is that it can be learned in a very short time, whereas it can take years of practice to read conventional music fluently. Its disadvantage is that it can only be used for one particular instrument, but for our purposes that doesn't matter.

If you're using the tablature, keep one eye on the music stems to glean the exact rhythm. Since the music and tablature are always vertically aligned this shouldn't be a problem (and consumer tests have borne this out). In a further effort to keep the layout uncluttered I've not included tied notes in the tablature, except where they cross bar lines; neither have I duplicated expression markings.

In the conventional music, left hand fingering is generally given at position shifts, and in any place where it may not be obvious. Sometimes it is given when the obvious may not be desirable: rather than playing up and down the neck, phrases often cross strings to wring the maximum sustain out of the mandolin. If in doubt, glance at the tablature.

It's worth remembering that two frets are generally covered by each finger of the left hand, but you'll find yourself having to break this rule on numerous occasions.

Although this is not meant to be a tutor book, I've explained various technical points - fingerings, position shifts and so forth. You can follow them closely if you want to know exactly how I play, otherwise treat them as suggestions. There's always more than one way to approach a tune. Rather than devote a separate section to technical matters, I've discussed them as they crop up.

# PREAMBLE

This book is a response to many kind requests from musicians who already have the Mandolin Albums on CD or cassette.

The recorded versions of these tunes are sometimes set in quite complex arrangements with a variety of other instruments, most notably the mandolin's bigger relatives, the mandola and mandocello. I never intended to transcribe these as if they were classical works cast in tablets of stone, but to present melody lines, harmonic structure and some technical guidance. Those so inspired will, I hope, create their own arrangements and variations.

If you're familiar with the recordings you'll notice a couple of omissions. These are cases where the complexity of the arrangements is as important to the tune's success as the melody line itself. Just a couple of these fully transcribed would fill a separate book, so I've saved them for a rainy day. In some cases I've presented slightly abridged versions which work better as solo pieces.

Some tunes were recorded on the lower instruments, but as the mandola and mandocello are less common I thought they would be more useful written out for the mandolin. If you wish you can always transpose down a fifth into alto clef for the mandola and down an octave and a fifth into bass clef for the mandocello. The tablature will be the same for all three instruments.

Finally, I'd like to thank Hilary James and Andy Baum, without whom ... etc.

Good Luck!

# The Buttermere Waltz

Simon Mayor

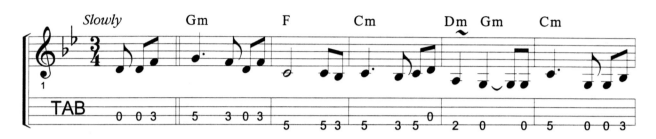

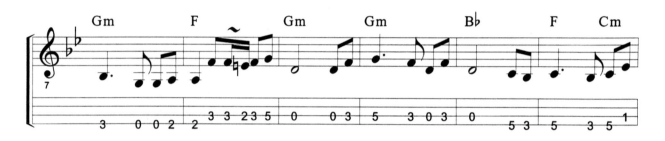

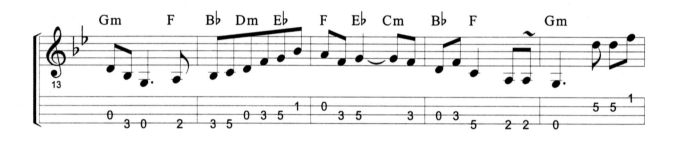

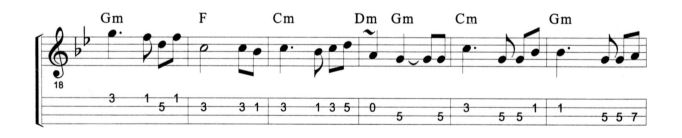

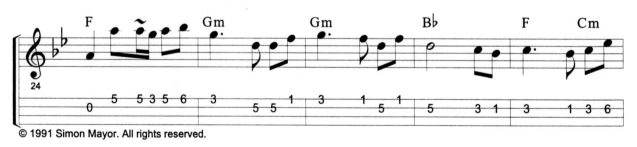

8

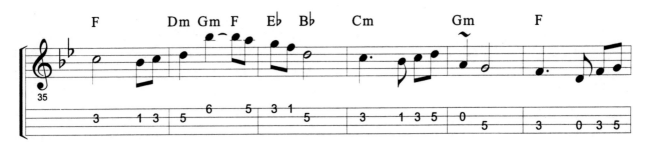

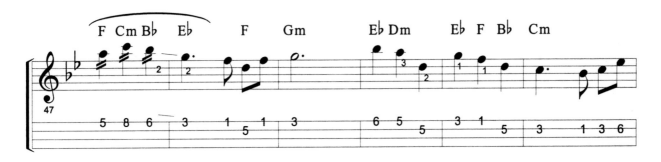

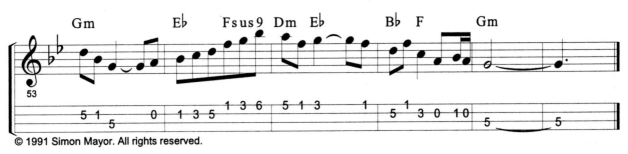

# Two Days In Tuscany

Simon Mayor

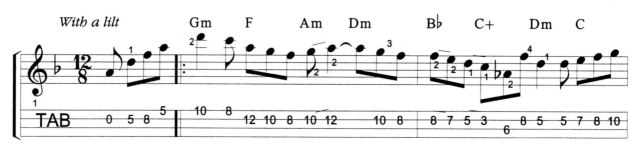

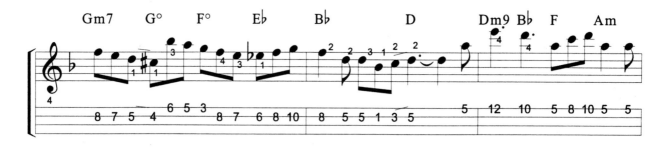

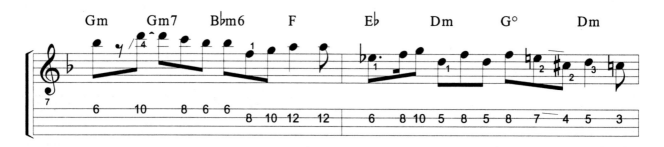

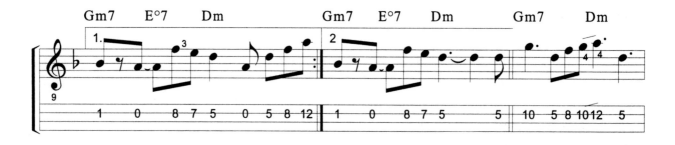

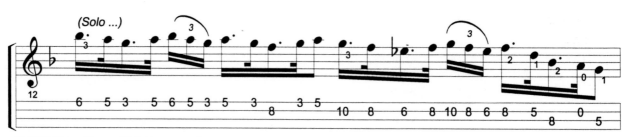

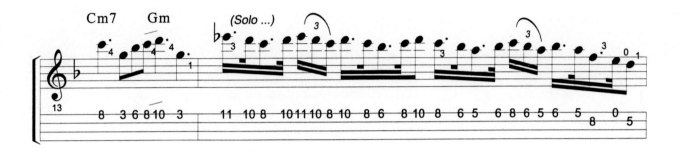

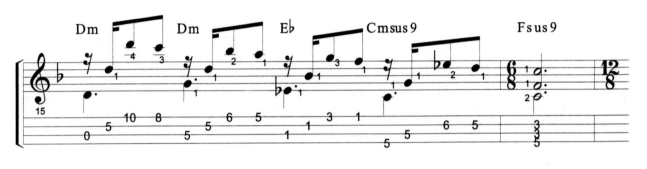

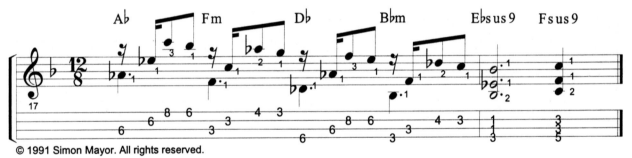

Unlike many tunes in this book the fingering does not make much use of string crossing. Don't be afraid to make a feature of all the position shifts by turning them into subtle glissandos - it gives the tune character.

# Dead Sea Dance (No. 1)

Simon Mayor

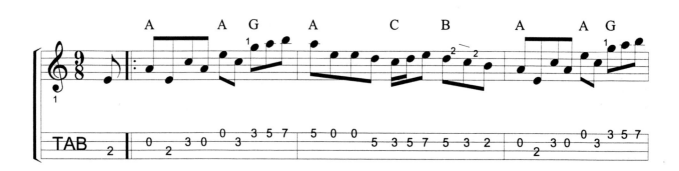

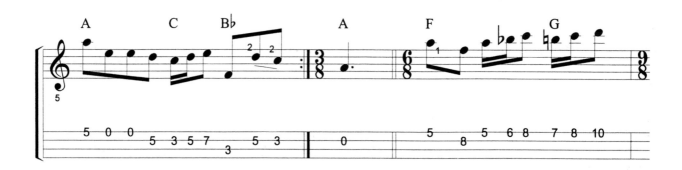

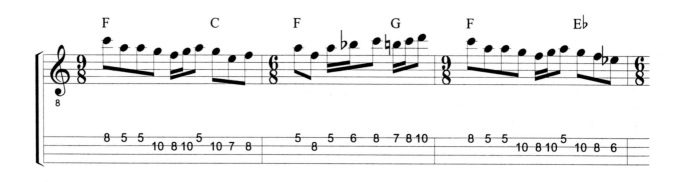

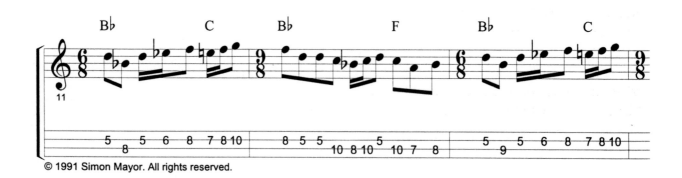

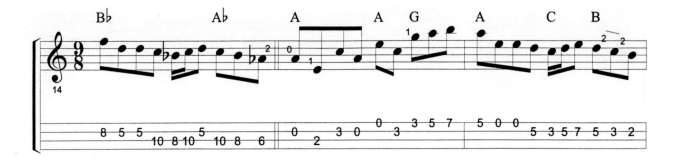

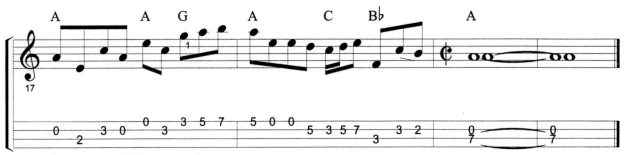

There's nothing technically too difficult about this, but the rhythm may be difficult to count. The bars of 9/8 are heavily accented on the 1st, 5th and 7th quavers. So the count goes 1-2-3-4, 1-2, 1-2-3. It's hypnotic when you get used to it, and similar to much Eastern European dance music.

This tune is particularly effective if played with another mandolinist playing the same thing transposed a fourth down. This produces an earthy harmony. Guitarists should leave the thirds out of the chords and stab the rhythm on the first of each group of beamed quavers. Dead Sea Dance No 2 should follow straight on....

# Dead Sea Dance (No. 2)

Simon Mayor

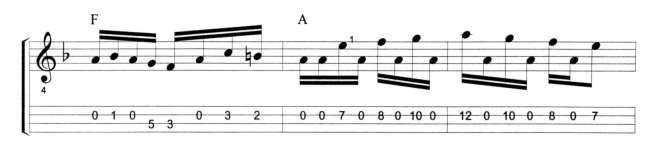

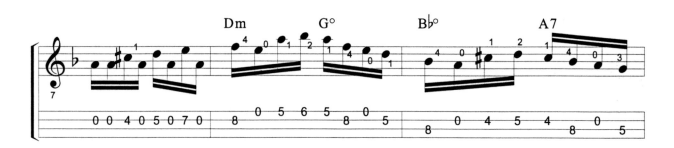

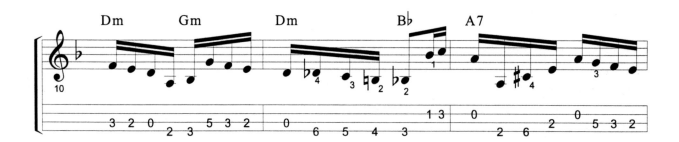

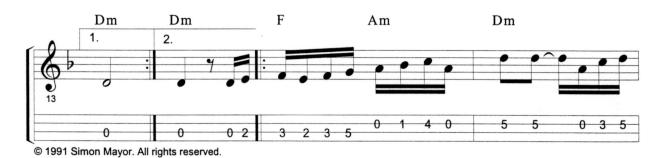

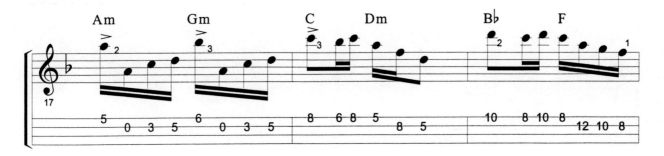

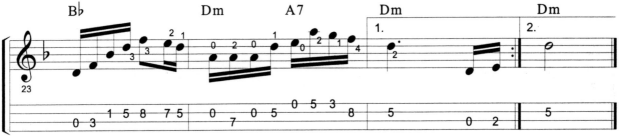

This is a very tricky tune to play fluently, so do make sure you've got the recommended position changes in your head before you play it at any speed. The rule of covering two frets with each finger goes right out of the window here, as a lot of the fingering is very bunched. You'll find it easier to play fluidly if you make good use of the little finger. As you become more familiar with it make liberal use of slides, pulloffs (try the triplet in bar 21) and all the tricks of the trade; it all adds character.

# Toss The Pancake

Simon Mayor

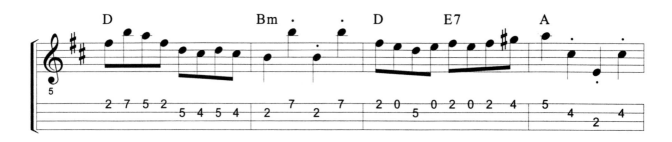

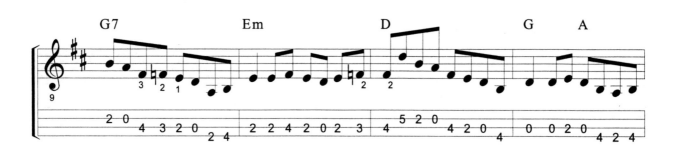

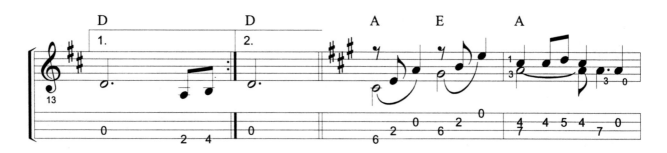

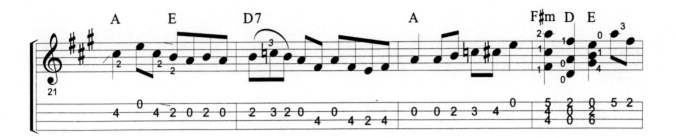

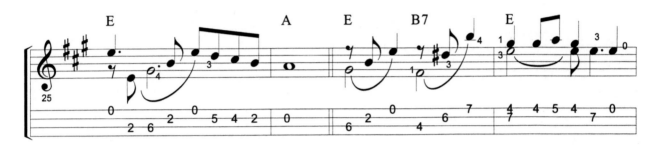

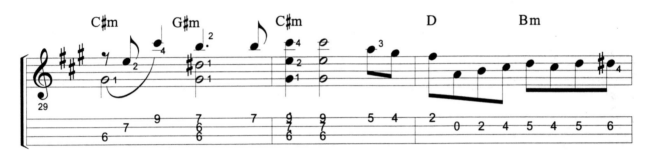

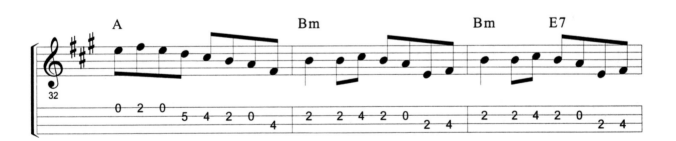

17

# Jump The Gun

Simon Mayor

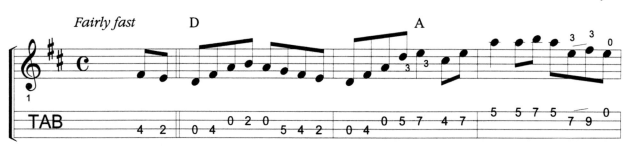

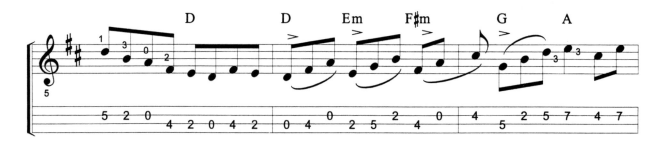

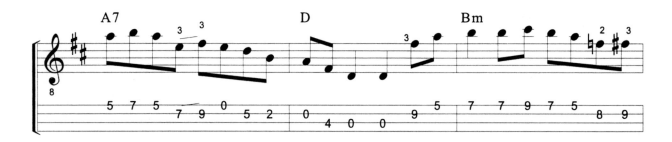

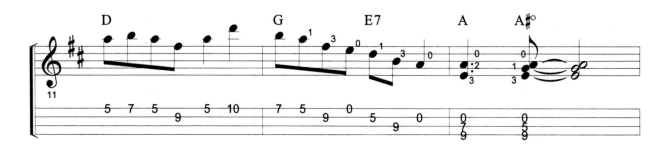

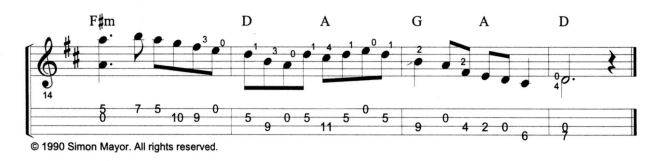

18

# THE THIRSTY MANDOLIN

Like most mandolinists, I started out on another instrument, and don't play the mandolin exclusively.

Some years ago I was celebrating a friend's birthday in the local pub. Several of us had been contributing a few tunes to the evening. My mandolin at the time was a modest Japanese factory built roundback. It cost £65 brand new in the mid-seventies, was beautifully made and played perfectly in tune right up to the 24th fret. A guitar maker opined at the time that he simply couldn't understand how the Japanese could produce it at such a price.

I digress. The hostelry was throbbing with a seething, stomping mass, encouraged in its appreciation by several barrels of Brakspear's bitter. Guitar in hand, I was hammering out a blues while the singer glued himself to the microphone to combat the hubbub. The mandolin lay on an adjacent table, unaware of the approaching pint wobbling towards it on the mantlepiece above. I glanced left and the world went into slow motion; the pint had reached the precipice and fell, gracefully emptying its every last drop into the soundhole. Yes, it was a direct hit with bitter consequences.

Those who have tasted the glory of Brakspear's will appreciate what a terrible waste this was. And the mandolin? It is dry now, but has a certain vintage odour associated with instruments many hundreds of years older. Of course, its tone lost all sparkle and the neck eventually warped. It now hangs on the wall, a pickle of its former self, a daily reminder of the evils of drink.

It has never had woodworm.

# Reelin' Over The Rooftops

Simon Mayor

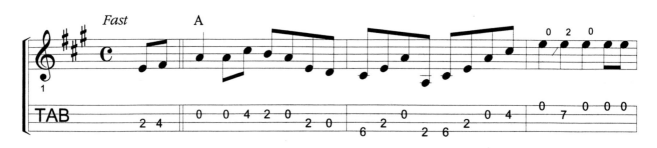

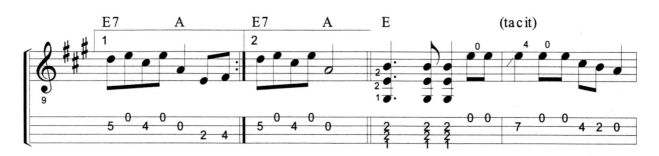

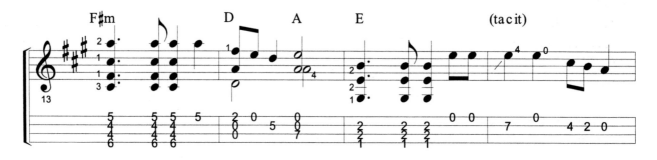

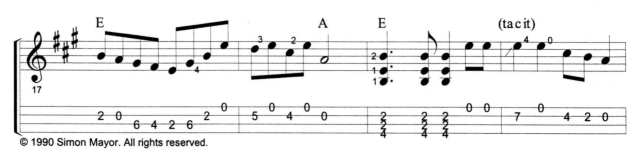

20

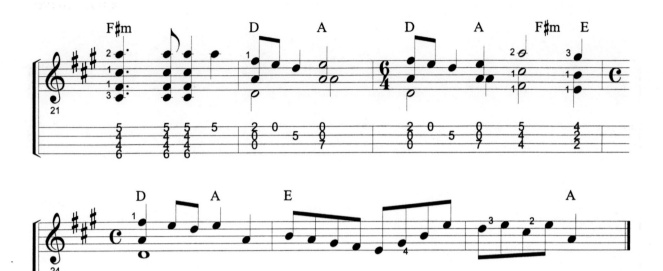

*Jump The Gun* and *Reelin' Over The Rooftops* were played as a medley.

There are two points to bear in mind with *Jump The Gun*. The rising triads in bars 6 and 7 can easily throw your rhythm, particularly as they involve syncopation and string crossing. The second section of the tune is played mostly in 3rd position, but using some open strings for a more harp like sustain. It may help to glance at the tablature as well as the music to take advantage of this effect.

You may like to increase speed when changing to *Reelin' Over The Rooftops*. Hold the left hand fingers down in bar 3 and the last four quavers of bars 17 and 25 to allow the arpeggios to ring. The chords in bars 11, 13, 15 and 21 can be played hard. The bar of 6/4 (bar 23) can be tricky for the rhythm guitarist. The F#m chord comes on the 5th beat of the bar and intentionally goes against the timing of the melody.

# The Mosstrooper Jig

Simon Mayor

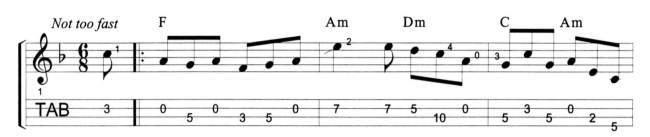

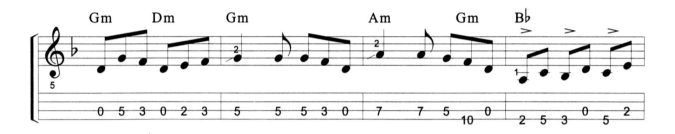

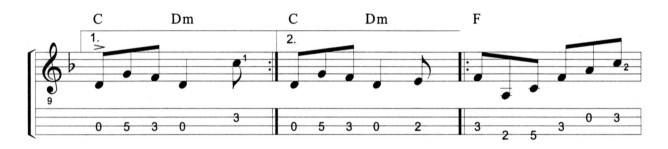

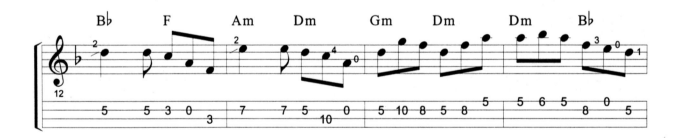

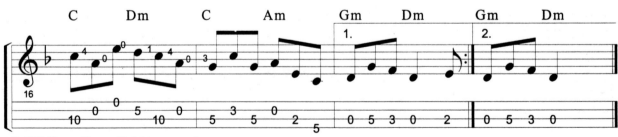

# The Mosstrooper March

Simon Mayor

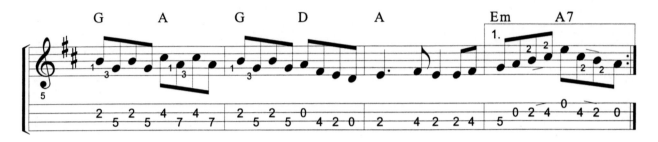

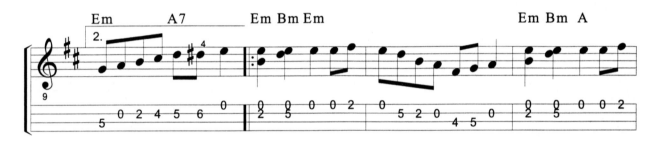

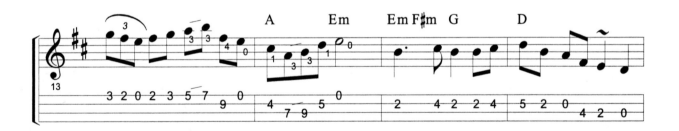

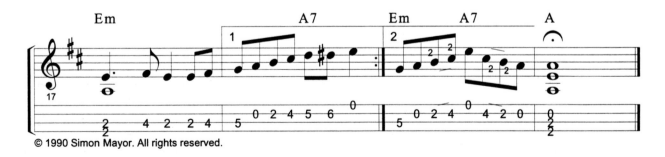

# The Mosstrooper Reel

Simon Mayor

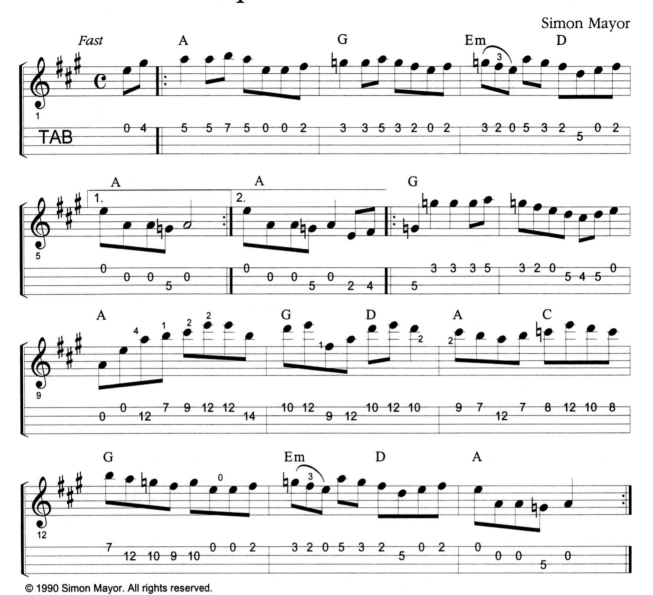

The three *Mosstrooper* tunes were recorded as a medley but there's no reason why they shouldn't be used individually.

As with some other tunes, the jig involves considerable string crossing to achieve a more sustained effect. You can help this along by keeping your fingers down on strings for as long as possible, allowing notes to ring underneath each other. This is generally a good habit to cultivate; the closer your fingers are kept to the fingerboard, even when they're not fretting anything, the more efficiently your left hand will operate. The reel should be taken reasonably briskly when you've got used to it. It was written and recorded on the guitar, but works fine on mandolin.

# PLECTRUMS

Tortoises, now a protected species, rejoice in not having to suffer leaky roofs just so that mandolinists can twang strings, and not before time. So tortoiseshell aside, it doesn't really matter what sort of plectrum you use.

My first efforts were with thin strips of whalebone stiffening taken from my shirt collars. These were as ecologically unsound as tortoiseshell of course, but at an early age the ethics of the matter never occured to me. My only advice now is to fork out the money and buy a commercially produced plectrum.

The artificial alternatives are plastic, nylon or a new carbon-reinforced nylon. Few would be able to tell the difference between these and tortoiseshell in a blindfold test. I have an irrational preference for plain ordinary plastic about 0.75mm thick, triangular with one pointed, and two rounded, corners. I find that this thickness and shape can give me a variety of tone colours: the point gives volume and clarity while the rounded corner gives a thicker tone particularly when slightly angled as it hits the strings. I generally try and strike the strings from a right-angle but *turning the plectrum* to about 45° means the plastic takes a split second longer to cross the strings. This thickens the tone considerably while still retaining the flexibility of a medium gauge plectrum. No matter what style you settle with, it's worth remembering that you should be able to vary the tone at will, so do experiment.

# Mad As A March Hare

Simon Mayor

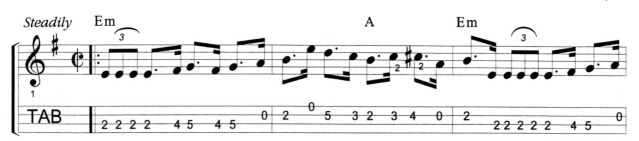

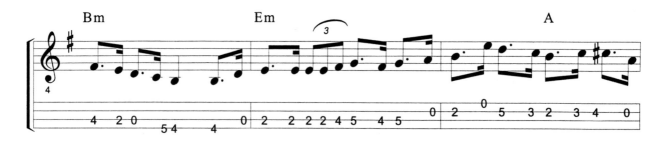

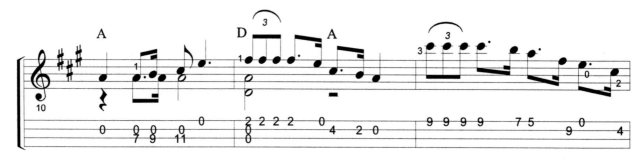

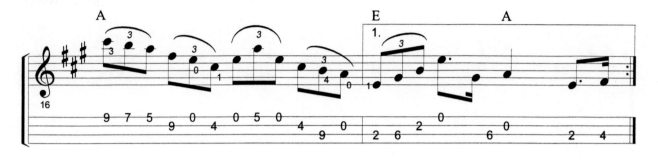

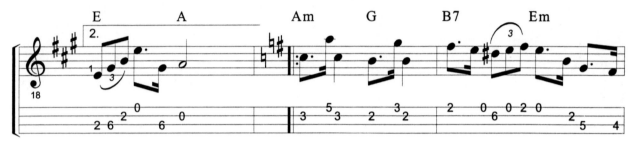

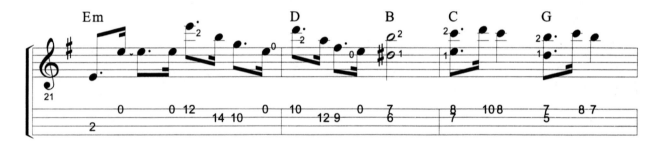

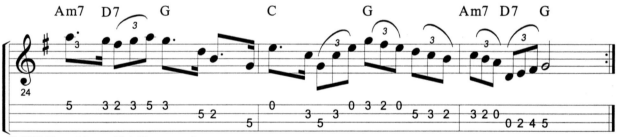

*Mad As A March Hare* is a whimsical ditty not meant to be played too quickly. Watch out for the first and fifth bars: the notes are exactly the same but the rhythm is different. The triplets in this tune are great exercise in plectrum control; read the rhythm carefully and don't be tempted to start out fast as you'll probably come a cropper at the end of the second section (bars 16 and 17).

A metronome might not go amiss for the first few runs through.

27

# Tune For A Mop Fair

Simon Mayor

This tune involves the left hand in a lot of tricky work getting round the chords, and is not easy on mandolins with narrow necks. Although with good guitar accompaniment it would suffice to play the melody line alone, the fuller version is far more effective. There are awkward moments. In bar 7 the third finger has to tuck quickly behind the fourth to get the D. Try and keep your fourth finger on the string as it slides it up to the B at the top of the next chord. A similar comment would apply to the third finger moving from the F# in bar 9 to the A in bar 10. In bar 34 you must release the first finger from the B immediately so the harmonic E rings clearly.

# The Hoppings

Simon Mayor

30

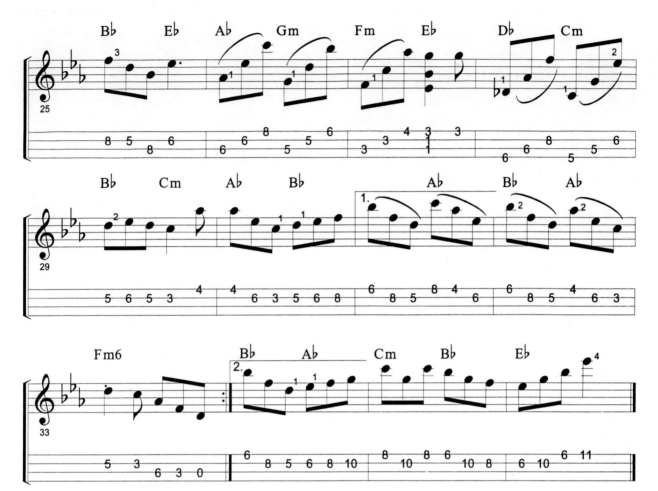

The Hoppings were - and still are - country dances held mostly in the North of England. They were originally organised by temperance societies out to prove that a good time could be had without alcohol. To this day they are dry, as many a musician faced with the tantalising choice of orange or lemon squash will testify.

The majority of folk dance tunes are in sharp keys (G, D, or A), the keys most suited to fiddles and of course mandolins. This jig started out life in D, but the low harmony I wanted to include in bars 5 and 18 demanded action, so up it went a semitone. It's certainly more of a finger-buster in this key, but great practice.

# Maple Flames

Simon Mayor

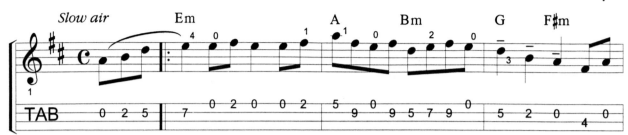

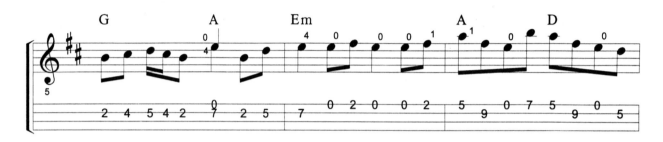

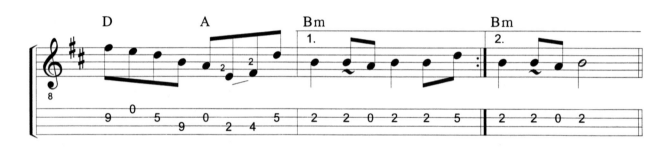

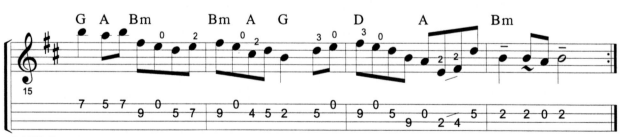

32

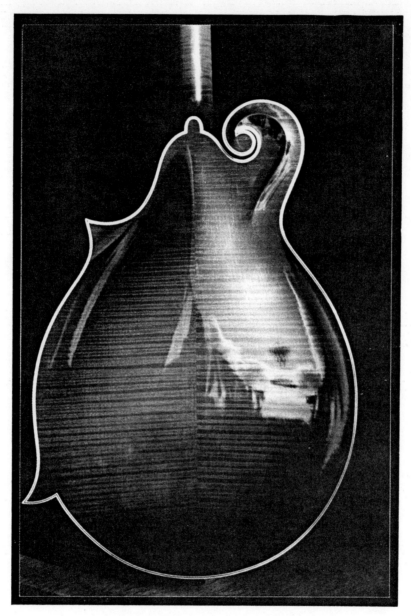

A mandola back made from a particularly
beautiful piece of flamed maple.

# The Exchange

Simon Mayor

This is a chordal arrangement of a Scottish-style air. It was originally played on the mandola where the lower pitch lends a more funereal atmosphere, and the slightly wider string spacing gives the fingers more room to get the chords in. Give the dotted rhythms great accent. The coda (overleaf) goes into double time, following more or less the same harmonies. Of course, if you use mandolin fingering on the mandola it will come out a fifth lower in C major.

# The Exchange - Coda

Simon Mayor

# Pipped At The Post

Simon Mayor

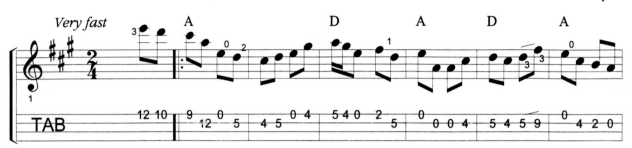

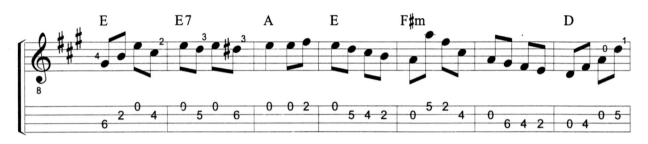

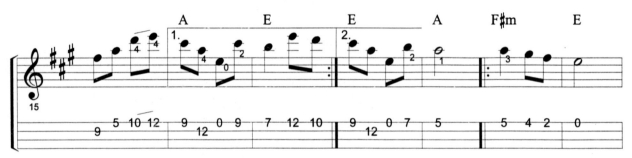

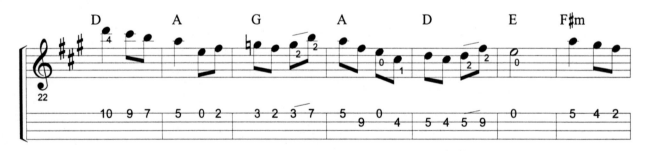

After writing *Jump The Gun* it seemed logical to follow it with *Pipped At The Post*. It turned out to be a very appropriate title as it usually finishes before I do. This is an extremely difficult tune venturing high up the neck. It should be played quite fast to be effective but as with all such things, you'll need to practise slowly.

There are a few things to bear in mind. In bar 4 play the high A with the plectrum and pull off the G and the open E with the left hand fingers. By snapping the string sideways as you release each finger you'll get three notes from one plectrum stroke.

If your left hand fingers are strong enough, there is no need to pick the F# in bar 6, the high E in bar 15 or the B in bar 24; slide hard from the previous note and with a bit of luck the mandolin should still be ringing.

Watch out for the use of open strings to aid position shifts, and don't be tempted to try getting the very last note just with a slide; it must be picked if you want a positive ending.

Great comic effect can be achieved by playing this last note a semitone sharp!

# The Jericho Waltz

Simon Mayor

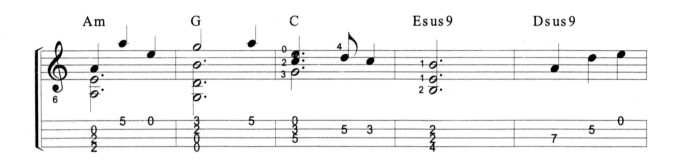

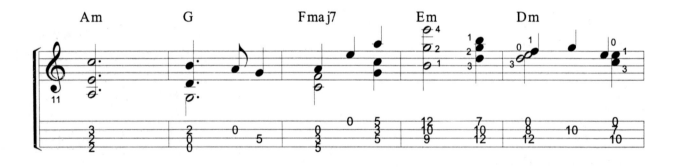

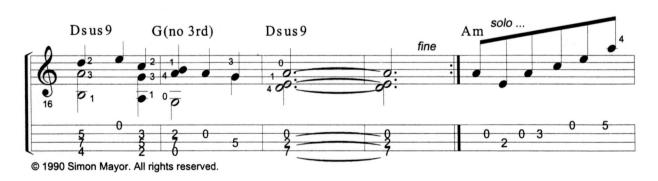

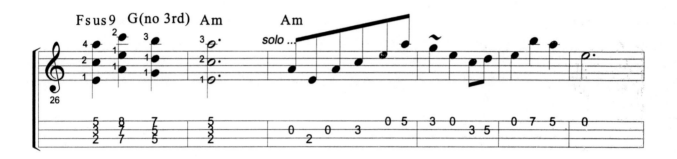

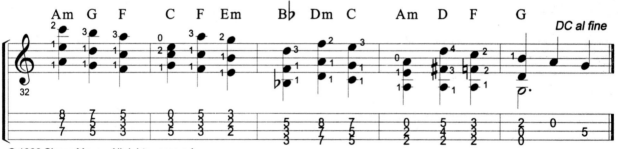

This tune makes use of quite fast moving chord changes, particularly in bars 32 - 36. It needs some very accurate left hand work if these are to be made cleanly.

# ROUNDBACK

There are two main sorts of mandolin, graced by descriptive titles.

The roundback is of Italian origin, played traditionally on one knee in the moonlight beneath windows of sweethearts.

Its body is made from strips of wood, steamed and bent into shape, and the top is 'broken' at the bridge position to allow a more acute angle of the strings. This places a greater downward force on the bridge and transmits vibrations to the body more efficiently. Nevertheless, its sound remains delicate but penetrating.

The round back renders it less than comfortable to play, especially to those blessed with a beer gut. Serious players will sometimes be seen draping chammy leather over it to stop it wobbling about (the instrument, not the gut). This instrument is played by virtually all classical players, and by those intent upon authenticity (my instrument is authentically 20th century).

Many roundbacks were taken over to America by Italian immigrants, but failed to stand up to the variable climate. The flatback was more than just an attempt to build a stronger instrument. It was a fundamental re-think, developed by the Gibson company in the USA early this century, the brainchild of their chief designer Lloyd Loar.

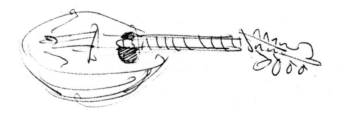

The design is very similar to a violin with the top and back carved into a gentle arch and the neck angled back to create pressure on the bridge. Over the years it has proved to be structurally stronger, particularly at the neck to body joint.

While the Italians were fond of covering their more expensive mandolins with acres of mother-of-pearl, Loar experimented more with the shape for cosmetic effect. Some had a simple tear-drop shape like their Italian ancestors, but he designed the now famous F5 model with the body outline swooping gracefully into decorative points and a scroll on the bass shoulder. Their protagonists claim the points and scroll add 'weight' to the sound while cynics refer to the scroll as the £1,000 strap button, for such is the premium in value over an 'A' model with its simple tear-drop shape.

F5s are traditionally played by bluegrass musicians. While enjoying the luxury of not having a round back wobbling out of control, they create other difficulties for themselves by slinging the strap over just one hunched shoulder. Style is everything! Love it or hate it, the Gibson F5 is *the* prestige mandolin to own if your musical diet extends beyond the strictly classical.

And the author? Well, when was the last time you heard of a Yorkshireman paying £1,000 for a strap button?

# Wheelin' & Dealin'

Simon Mayor

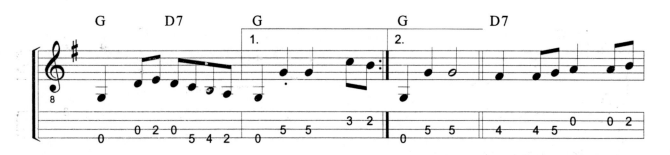

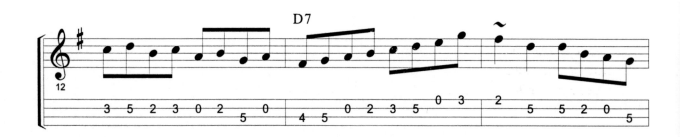

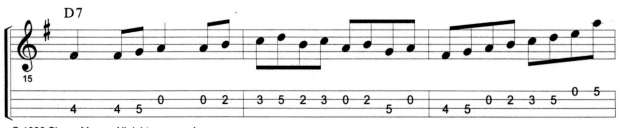

44

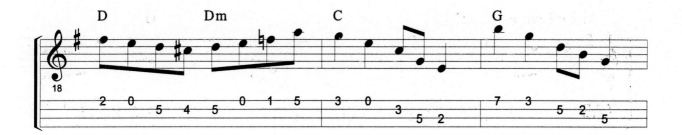

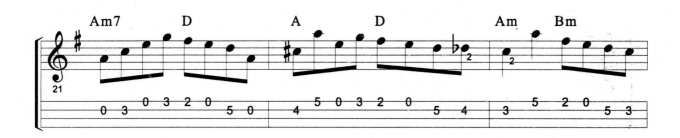

A cheeky ditty with nothing particularly difficult about it. Play it with a bouncy feel and perhaps dot the rhythm a little.